# CONFLICT RESOLUTION FOR KIDS

# CONFLICT RESOLUTION FOR KIDS

## A Group Facilitator's Guide

Pamela S. Lane

ACCELERATED DEVELOPMENT

*A member of the Taylor & Francis Group*

| | | |
|---|---|---|
| **USA** | Publishing Office: | ACCELERATED DEVELOPMENT<br>*A member of the Taylor & Francis Group*<br>1101 Vermont Ave., N.W., Suite 200<br>Washington, DC 20005<br>Tel: (202) 289-2174<br>Fax: (202) 289-3665 |
| | Distribution Center: | ACCELERATED DEVELOPMENT<br>*A member of the Taylor & Francis Group*<br>1900 Frost Road, Suite 101<br>Bristol, PA 19007-1598<br>Tel: (215) 785-5800<br>Fax: (215) 785-5515 |
| **UK** | | Taylor & Francis, Ltd.<br>4 John Street<br>London WC1N 2ET<br>Tel: 071 405 2237<br>Fax: 071 831 2035 |

**CONFLICT RESOLUTION FOR KIDS: A Group Facilitator's Guide**

1 2 3 4 5 6 7 8 9 0 BRBR 0 9 8 7 6 5

This book was set in Times Roman by Taylor & Francis. Technical development by Cynthia Long. Prepress Supervisor was Miriam Gonzalez. Cover design by Michelle Fleitz. Printing and binding by Braun-Brumfield, Inc.

A CIP catalog record for this book is available from the British Library.

∞ The paper in this publication meets the requirements of the ANSI Standard Z39.48-1984 (Permanence of Paper)

**Library of Congress Cataloging-in-Publication Data**
Lane, Pamela, S.
   Conflict resolution for kids: a group facilitaor's guide/Pamela S. Lane.
      p. cm.
   Includes bibliographical references.

   1. Conflict management—Study and teaching. 2. Interpersonal conflict in children—Study and teaching.
   3. Group work in education. I. Title.
HM136.L3722 1995                                      95-12459
303.6'9'07—dc20                                        CIP

ISBN 1-56032-387-6

# TABLE OF CONTENTS

# LIST OF ACTIVITIES

# LIST OF FIGURES

# INTRODUCTION

In the violent and litigious atmosphere of our society, many who work with children search for the means to make a difference. Family violence, overcrowded prisons, and the increasingly younger age of gang members all testify to the fact that conflict—and our inability to deal with it—should be a focal point for those professionals working with children.

Do our children get the message about conflict? Only too well. TV and film tell them that conflict is resolved through loss of blood on the street and loss of money in court. How can we counteract this message? Many schools and community health centers have chosen to take on jobs formerly done by families (Koch, 1988; Maxwell, 1989). Conflict resolution is now being taught in schools throughout our nation. Although the forum may not be as attractive or enticing as those that exist in the movie theaters, conflict resolution may be a more personal one. Students who are exposed to, taught, and given opportunity to practice different strategies for resolving interpersonal disputes may have more of a chance to avoid violence in their lives--even for the simple reason that they know another way. Reacting to conflict situations might become a matter of choosing a familiar strategy that seems appropriate to the situation at hand.

## THE GROUP

An opportunity to personalize this process lies in the group experience where an atmosphere of "acceptance, encouragement, and safe exploration for new behaviors" can be created (Morganett, 1990, p. 1). As we know, peers strongly influence children, and a task oriented group builds on the premise that the young people will attempt, practice, and model behaviors for one another (Gazda, Asbury, Childers, & Walters, 1977).

The group format allows a focus on feelings and the resolution of affective issues as well as conflict resolution. In this setting, children not only can experiment with various strategies for dispute resolution, but they also can process their emotional reaction to the use of the techniques. In the group's acknowledgment of the fact that not every way of resolving conflict works for every child at all times, permission is given for uniqueness of the individual's emerging interpersonal style and development of intrapersonal philosophy regarding conflict.

A group approach to conflict resolution for children can be a **therapeutic group** (for children with behavioral problems) or a **growth group** (for children who are functioning normally). A conflict resolution group for children may be **preventive** or **remedial** in nature. Whatever its purpose, a conflict resolution training group for children will have a strong guidance component, as it will be necessary to guide members in their discovery of the many strategies that are available for resolving disputes. Physical activities may serve to illustrate a cognitive concept. Role-play may give the children a chance to "feel" the tension of conflict and the "pride" of competence when an issue is resolved mutually and successfully. The group provides a safe and nurturing atmosphere in which to process "what happened" and "how I felt about it."

An outlined approach—a kind of facilitator's guidebook—to the implementation of a conflict resolution experiential group for children is what follows. In the setting where this group was implemented initially, the "parent connection" was highly valued. Thus, "homework" activities were designed to share information and experiences with family members. Parents attended the first half-hour of both the first and the last of the group's five sessions. A closed group format was chosen as best for this specific setting; however, in another setting, a children's conflict resolution group could be converted easily to an open-ended group (Yalom, 1985).

## NOTE TO THE GROUP FACILITATOR

If you are a counselor, teacher, or other professional who is contemplating the facilitation of a Conflict Resolution Group for children, you may have concerns with respect to the amount of leader preparation and ongoing energy output that might be required by the organizational demands of such an undertaking; I would like to offer encouragement in this area.

*Conflict Resolution for Kids* is a group that requires minimal leader preparation and delegates much of the "group business"--procedural things--to the group members themselves. The structure soon to be described allows you, the facilitator, to observe the members' interactions, take advantage of spontaneous conflicts that may occur in the life of the group, incorporate your favorite video with problem-solving themes, and empower children with conflict resolution strategies developed in your own "lab" group setting.

The five sessions can and have changed family interactions, have strengthened child self-esteem, and have provided children with "tools" to use in their future, inevitable experiences with conflict. My observation of this process has been that the facilitator's energy output is at its greatest for Session One, and thereafter, with the structure in place, the group becomes "self-propelled." You, the facilitator, provide the discovery materials and activities that are all included in this guide and that may be integrated with some of your tried and true activities that are already in your repertoire.

The enthusiasm of children, their parents, and referring professionals has taught me something about the importance of providing this group. Being a member of a Conflict Resolution for Kids group carries no stigma. Conflict is a natural part of all our lives. Both "regular" and "special needs" children have participated and benefited. This group develops in settings where inclusion might be considered enrichment or prevention as well as in settings where referral to *Conflict Resolution for Kids* might serve a rehabilitative or therapeutic function. Group members benefit from the socialization focusing on responsibility for one's own emotions, thinking and behavioral choices, teamwork, problem ownership, cooperative task focus, and acceptance of individual differences.

The youngest children may say, "The group is fun!" Developmentally more mature participants may have great lists of conflict resolution strategies learned and attitudinal adjustments made. When you evaluate your group's progress, you may find that members differ in their expression of gains, and if you have used the suggested multi-age grouping of sub-teams, this is an appropriate outcome. To assist you in your preparation, facilitation, and evaluation phases, each session script lists materials required, presentation sequence suggestions, evaluation considerations, and assessment instruments. Your personal reflections on the experience are solicited by the author, and a facilitator evaluation is included at the back of the book to convey your thoughts and feelings.

I think you will find *Conflict Resolution for Kids* a helpful guide in providing a valuable opportunity for the children you serve, whether your setting be public school, social service/mental health agency, or community youth organization. Have fun teaching what may be the most important skills children in today's world need to learn!

## THE FACILITATOR'S PROCESS

1. Group advertisement (Figure 1)

2. Sign up

3. Parent or guardian consent and commitment forms (Figure 6)

4. Assignment of members to "sub-teams" within the group (by age, sex, siblings)

5. Pre-group survey regarding attitude toward conflict (Figures 4 and 5)

6. Group facilitation (five sessions, five weeks)

7. Children's demonstration of skills for families

8. Post-group survey (Figures 4 and 5)

9. Evaluation of experience

# CONFLICT RESOLUTION FOR KIDS
# GROUP FORMING

*Parents: Would you like a more peaceful home life?*
*If your children's arguing is getting you down,*
*this group experience might be just the one to make a difference!*

Conflict Resolution for Kids

will meet on the following five _____,

from _____ to _____

at _____(location)

**Parents are requested to attend**

**the first one-half hour on _____,**

**and families are cordially invited to the**

**Conflict Manager graduation ceremony on the last group night.**

*Your child (children) will have the opportunity to*
*Learn & Practice Dispute Resolution Skills*
*Communicate Effectively using*
*Reflective Listening*
*Respectful Assertion*
*Issue Identification*
*and Make Friends and Have Fun!*

**Sign up soon. Limited capacity. Call _____ to register.**

**It's a fun way to *Give Peace a Chance!***

**Figure 1.** Announcement used to advertise the formation of a conflict resolution group.

## PRE- AND POST-GROUP ASSESSMENT

The conflict survey designed by Schmidt and Friedman (1985) is appropriate for older children (see Figure 5). It is written at approximately a fourth-grade reading level. A simpler pre-group measure designed for a second grader's comfort may be facilitator-created or found in Figure 4. The purposes of the pre- and post-group surveys are twofold: to aid the group facilitator in evaluating the extent to which ideas about conflict were broadened as a result of the group, and to allow children to become aware of their personal growth in their attitudes toward conflict.

## GROUP OBJECTIVES

Goals for a children's conflict resolution experiential group may be summarized as follows:

- to create an awareness of the many strategies available for resolving conflict;

- to empower group members with confidence through practicing of clear communication skills to be used in dispute resolution;

- to utilize children's actual experiences in conflict resolution role-plays;

- to concretize concepts like anger management, specific communication, listening skills, and reflective attending through activities;

- to involve parents in a support role at home through the use of background information packets, contracts, and "home work" assignments; and

- to offer group members a safe, nurturing environment in which to try new behaviors and process their feelings about their experiences.

If the "family connection" is an identified value to the facilitator, given the setting, then an effort to outline objectives in a behavioral way may be advantageous. These goals may be communicated to the parents/guardians in a pre-group meeting or in a handout similar to the "Parent Page" (Figure 7).

## GROUP COMPOSITION

The recommended number is six to eight members (Yalom, 1985); however, the number may vary if you as facilitator subgroup the members into "sub-teams." However, groups of more than ten may experience diminishing returns. Teams of three children can easily work on role-plays together, do a "team task" that then contributes in an additive fashion to the group process, divide and distribute snacks while managing conflict, and observe while another team acts. Flexibility is built in when these subgroups or teams are created. They may be dropped or reassumed as the moment requires. Whatever you decide, the recommendation is that there be ritual in that decision's use and attention to the ritual's regular presence. For example, team leaders can take attendance for their subgroup, serve snacks, and communicate with the facilitator regarding needs, problems, or questions. In five sessions, each member of a subgroup or team can be "leader" at least once. This "task" orientation, although not usual for a counseling group, is especially important in establishing the safety, security of routine, and atmosphere of trust desirable. These "tangibles," which are unnecessary when facilitating adult groups, are essential in children's groups.

In the composing of children's groups, a warning is sometimes issued (Morganett, 1990) regarding inclusion of siblings. In a conflict resolution training group, it is desirable to have brothers and sisters in the same group, though in different "teams" or subgroups. Siblings represent an immediate source of conflict in most children's lives, and watching them resolve role-play conflicts with other team members gives the observing sibling opportunity for insight and perhaps a new perspective.

Some children's group facilitators prefer to work with family members of nearly the same age. It can be argued that difference in age and interest adds dimension to a task and process group where the focus is conflict. The older members often model skill levels, which benefits younger members. Younger members are often less inhibited than older members and model a level of "unself-consciousness" helpful to the climate of the group. Older members have an opportunity to empathize with the problems of the younger members and are often "drawn out" in the process of "reaching out." For example, in a conflict resolution training group for kids advertised for elementary-age children, the age range could be from approximately 6 to 13. If this range is present, it becomes important to formulate subgroups or teams with children from a mixture of age groups represented. In a conflict resolution group of nine members aged 6 to 12, the subgroups shown in Figure 2 could be devised. Subgrouping encourages role-play, task focus, and ease of participation for reticent members, and promotes opportunity for the rotation of team leadership offering more modeling moments.

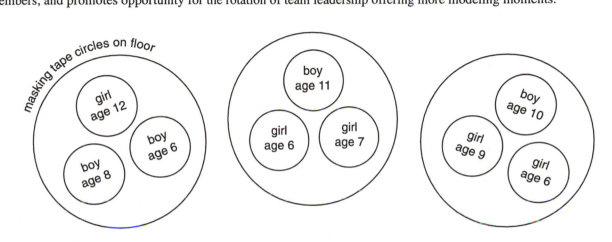

**Figure 2.** Suggested "sub-teaming" of nine children in a conflict resolution group.

## THE SETTING

With respect to physical setting, a small, carpeted room with plenty of wall space for poster display (see Figure 3) is a good choice. Masking tape circles on the floor defining seating space for each team is a way members can feel comfortable each week--always knowing where their spots will be. As members enter the room for the sessions, one ritual may be finding your name tag in your team circle, putting it on, and sitting in the circle while the team leader-of-the-week takes attendance. Chairs may be used for role-play situations but should be disregarded as the usual seating arrangement for the children because chairs interfere with the freedom of movement and activity that are important parts of children's group experience.

A snack station with refreshments for break can be visited by the team leader who serves team members so as to resolve any conflict that might arise over who gets how many of what. The facilitator may wish to have sacks of crackers prepared for each team. Each sack might contain a number of crackers that does not equal the number of members in the team--thus creating a mini-opportunity for conflict resolution. A fun task can be to resolve snack time in a different way each session. This is just one of the activity ideas that are summarized in the Session Scripts.

**Figure 3.** Poster ideas.

## SESSION SCRIPTS

A session-by-session facilitator guide in script form is provided. Activities have been gathered from many sources. The Tug-of-War activity (1.6) and the Tied-Up-in-Knots activity (1.8) were originated by Schmidt and Friedman (1985). The role-plays for use in Activity 3.3 and Activity 3.6 were in part generated by group members and by the author. When materials are intended for reproduction by the facilitator, they are located as "Figure ___" immediately after the activity in which they are intended to be used or at the end of the session.

# SESSION ONE

**Materials Required for Session One**

- name tags (different colors for separate sub-teams)
- masking tape circles on the floor (indicating sub-team seating area)
- snacks (packaged crackers) on nearby table
- duplicated material (prepared prior to Session One):
    - Pre-group Surveys (Figures 4 and 5)
    - Parent/Guardian Consent and Commitment Forms (Figure 6)
    - Parent Page (Figure 7)
    - Conflict Logs (cover to be photocopied and stapled to blank paper pages [Figure 8])
- one tug-of-war rope (soft, kind to hands...from fabric store)
- posters showing conflict resolution options (Figure 3)
- poster with words to a ritual closing song such as "Let There Be Peace on Earth"

**Session Time: 1 1/2 Hours**

**Goals for Session One**

- to establish comfort level/rapport (parents and children considered),
- to convey purpose of the group,
- to establish "fun" climate of learning by doing,
- to engender commitment to all five sessions (parents and children), and
- to establish norms for group member behavior.

# ACTIVITIES FOR SESSION ONE

**First 30 Minutes**

---
### Activity 1.1  GETTING OFF TO A GOOD START
---

Welcome parents and children; help children find name tags; have children sit in team circles.  Parents sit in chairs on each of which is placed the "Parent Page" (handout shown in Figure 7), which they will take home to read at their leisure.

---
### Activity 1.2  ADMINISTRATING DETAILS
---

After explaining what the group is about, ask parents to read the "Consent Form" and the "Commitment Form" (Figure 6), sign them, and return them to you. In Figure 6, a parent or guardian signs a commitment to the effect that the child will attend all five sessions and bring his/her "Conflict Log" to each session with a recorded observation of a conflict complete.  Be sure to have children and parents decide where, at home, the "Conflict Log" (Figure 8) will be kept.

---

### Activity 1.3  INTRODUCING THE GROUP CONCEPT

---

When introducing the group concept to the parents and children, an illustrative example may be to tell the story of the three blind men who were touching an elephant to discover what it looked like--one at the tail, one at the trunk, and one at the ear. Each was describing the same animal, and each had a very different description. So it is with conflict. In an argument, we often are talking about the same thing, but we have different perspectives. We often have conflicts around the same truth, but we each have a singular hold on a piece of it. It may be helpful to tell the parents and children that one of our goals is to recognize that each person involved in a conflict has his/her perspective. We will try to grasp the idea that each person has his/her own truth, and as we learn our strategies, we will practice them with an awareness of individual differences and perspectives. Parents may see how this focus of the group can help them at home when they are in conflict with their child and have very different perspectives 5 on an issue.

---

### Activity 1.4  COMPLETING THE PRE-GROUP SURVEY

---

Have the children complete the "Pre-group Survey." If a child is younger (6 to 10 years of age), use Figure 4; if a child is older (11 to 12 years of age), use Figure 5. Save the responses for post-group comparison at the end of five sessions.

**Remaining 1 Hour**

---

### Activity 1.5  GETTING TO KNOW YOU

---

After the parents leave is a good time for a getting-to-know-you activity. Each child can take a turn telling his/her name, age, school, etc., and what conflict "bugs" him/her the most. Children will be restless after the introduction. It must be time to get up and move around!

---

### Activity 1.6  TUG-OF-WAR

---

Have everyone get up and take a position on the "user-friendly" rope. Instruct members to think: What kinds of problems are best solved in a competitive way? Then everyone pulls until one side wins.

---

### Activity 1.7  TIME TO PROCESS

---

Interview the losers with the following questions:

1. How does it feel to lose?
2. What if there had to be a winner and a loser after every conflict?
3. What if you were always the loser?
4. Are there other ways to resolve conflict that do not end up with losers?

---

### Activity 1.8  TIED-UP-IN-KNOTS

---

This time, the group watches as two members are "tied up" loosely by the facilitator. Before being given the signal to get untied, the two children and the group are given a think cue: What kinds of problems are best resolved through cooperation? The two then help each other unscramble themselves. Some discover the value of verbal communication in solving the problem.

---

### Activity 1.9  TIME TO PROCESS

---

Interview both participant with the following questions:

1. How did you feel working together?
2. Was anyone the loser?
3. Did anyone get hurt?
4. What might have happened if you hadn't worked together?

---

### Activity 1.10  ENJOYING SNACK TIME WITH MINI-CONFLICT

---

Snack time can be organized in such a way as to create opportunity for conflict in the sub-teams. The team leaders bring the crackers or cookies to their team members (pre-prepared bags of goodies—an insufficient number of items to go around). Each team leader facilitates the discussion on generating options for a fair and workable resolution of the problem. Children can be encouraged to solve the snack problem in a new way each session.

---

### Activity 1.11  EXPLANATION OF CONFLICT LOGS

---

In the last 15 minutes of this session, review expectations regarding "Conflict Logs." Tell members to watch for some conflicts they can observe this week. What was the problem? What did those involved do? How do you think they felt? Draw or write. Remind children to bring their Logs to the next session.

---

**Activity 1.12  CLOSING RITUAL**

---

The sessions may be ended in the same way every time.  Closure can be the singing of a song of peace like "Let There Be Peace on Earth" or another song with a similar message.

## EVALUATION CONSIDERATIONS (WHAT TO LOOK FOR)

Was the group structure/routine established?  Will the children know their fellow sub-team members next time, will they expectantly sit in their circles, will team leaders immediately begin to take attendance, and did all group members leave with Conflict Logs in hand, planning to record incidents of conflict and bring them back to group next week?  If so, you probably have established a highly motivating climate and one in which the structure will be comfortably familiar upon members' return.

Was each child involved in some aspect of Session One?  Perhaps it was the tug-of-war, perhaps it was the survey, perhaps it was resolving the mini-conflict at snack time.  As long as each child was engaged around some element of Session One, then you can be assured that "What the group's about" is beginning to unfold for the children.  Keep your eye on "engagement" with the materials, activities, leader, and other members.  Those who have an ongoing interchange with the elements of the experience will benefit the most.

**CONFLICT**

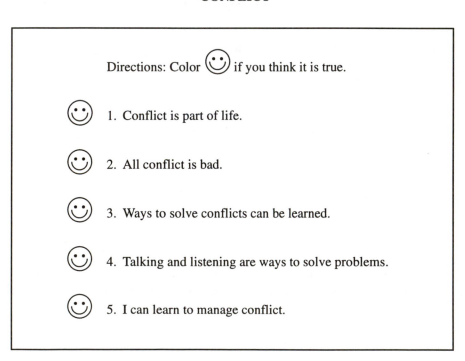

**Figure 4.**   Pre- and post-group survey for younger children (ages 6 to 10).   (Permission to photocopy is granted.)

**CONFLICT**

Directions:  Read each statement carefully.

Circle T if you think the statement is true and F if you think it is false.

T       F        1.  Conflict is a natural part of life.

T       F        2.  All conflicts end in violence.

T       F        3.  There are at least two sides in every conflict.

T       F        4.  It is possible to eliminate conflict.

T       F        5.  Behavior can be either appropriate or inappropriate depending on where it happens.

T       F        6.  Inappropriate behavior can cause conflict.

T       F        7.  Behavior cannot be changed.

T       F        8.  People all over the world have the same basic needs.

T       F        9.  Unmet needs can cause a conflict.

T       F       10.  There are many nonviolent alternatives available to solve a conflict.

T       F       11.  It is not possible for everyone to win in a conflict.

T       F       12.  Calling someone a name is a form of violence.

T       F       13.  Frustration always leads to violence.

T       F       14.  It is important to learn not to get angry.

T       F       15.  Adults never have conflicts.

T       F       16.  Conflict can be constructive as well as destructive.

T       F       17.  Conflicts can escalate or de-escalate, depending on what is said or done.

T       F       18.  Fighting fair means respect for others and for ourselves.

T       F       19.  In resolving a conflict it is important not to embarrass or humiliate the other person.

T       F       20.  Learning to handle conflict constructively takes a lot of practice and skill.

**Figure 5.**   Pre- and post-group survey for older children (ages 11 and 12).  Is included here with permission from Grace Cotrino Abrams Peace Education Foundation and was developed by Schmidt and Friedman (1985).  (Permission to photo-copy is granted.)

## PARENT/GUARDIAN CONSENT FORM

Your permission is requested for _____ to participate in group life skills development activities facilitated by _____ taking place on five consecutive _____ in the months of _____, from _____ to _____ each _____ until _____ when there will be a "Conflict Manager" Graduation Ceremony to which parents/guardians are invited. The group meetings will be held in _____.

The group is entitled CONFLICT RESOLUTION FOR KIDS and will include discussion of ideas, behaviors, feelings, attitudes, and opinions. Explored will be many strategies for managing disputes that occur in the normal course of daily living.

Participants will have the opportunity to learn new skills and behaviors that may help their personal development and adjustment.

The group will be facilitated by _____.

Information shared by group members will be kept confidential except in certain situations in which there is an ethical responsibility to limit confidentiality. In the following circumstances reporting is mandated:

If your child reveals information about hurting himself/herself or another

If your child reveals information about child abuse

If your child reveals information about criminal activity

- - - - - - - - - - - - - - - - - - - - - - - - - - - - - - - - - - - - - - - - - - - - - - - - - - - - - - - - - - - - - - - - - - - - - - - - - - - - - -

By signing this form, I give my informed consent for my child (children) to participate in the above described group. I understand that

1. The group will provide an opportunity for members to learn and practice interpersonal skills, discuss feelings, share ideas, practice new behaviors, and make new friends.

2. Anything group members share in group will be kept confidential by the group leader except in the above mentioned cases.

PARENT/GUARDIAN: _____ DATE: _____

CHILD (CHILDREN): _____

**Figure 6.** Consent form to be completed by parent or guardian. (Permission to photocopy is granted.)

## PARENT/GUARDIAN COMMITMENT FORM


I _____ promise to help my child remember to take his/her Conflict Log to every group meeting.  We will discuss a safe place to always keep it.


_____ (place we agreed upon)


I will help him/her record (draw or write) one observed conflict situation in the Conflict Log to bring to the next group session for discussion.  I will encourage him/her to consult his/her Strategy Wheel when resolving conflicts at home and to take his/her Strategy Wheel to each group meeting.


_____          _____

signature: parent or guardian                      child witness


_____

signature: parent or guardian


**Figure 6 (continued).**  Commitment form to be completed by parent or guardian.  (Permission to photocopy is granted.)

## PARENT PAGE

**Why a Conflict Group?**

It is natural for brothers, sisters, neighbors, and school mates to argue. In fact, conflict (what most adults and many children dread) is a natural part of daily life.

If disagreements always will be with us, then it makes sense that we learn how to deal with them effectively--causing little or no injury to life, limb, and self-esteem.

Conflict absorbs a lot of energy in the home and school. Young people who have a number of strategies for interpersonal problem solving are less likely to choose fighting as a solution because there are so many more effective alternatives. Having many "tools" to do the job also builds confidence in one's ability to handle future difficult disputes.

Think about the conflicts in adult lives--between partners, fellow workers, and neighbors. If you feel tense and frustrated when you are faced with such situations, you can be fairly sure your child feels similar frustration when dealing with conflict in his/her own life. Though it is not possible to eliminate conflict from our lives, it is possible to "manage" it in ways that may change how we feel about problem solving. With some new experiences it may be possible to view conflict as a chance to use creativity, a motivator for change, and an opportunity for personal growth. Conflict happens when individuals have different perspectives on an issue. Through they may feel "very far apart," they are actually "together" in that they both have a common interest in resolving the problem.

*Conflict Resolution for Kids* is a group designed to assist your children in becoming able to "see" another's perspective, to use appropriate strategies, and, when possible, to generate options cooperatively that may resolve the dispute. Your family may experience a change in emotional climate during the next five weeks. Watch for emerging Conflict Managers' use of some of these strategies for solving problems at home:

| | |
|---|---|
| • Using Humor | • Postponing |
| • Cooperating | • Getting Help |
| • Listening | • Communicating |
| • Taking Turns | • Avoiding |
| • Sharing | • Mediating |
| • Using Chance | |

**Figure 7.** Parent Page to be distributed during Session One. (Permission to photocopy is granted.)

_____
NAME

# CONFLICT LOG

- Homework:  Observe this week the conflicts happen-
             ing around you and those in which you
             are involved.

             What strategy did they (you) use to
             resolve the problem?

             Write in your log a few lines (or draw a
             picture) about the conflicts you observed
             . . . then share one example with the
             group next session.

**Take me with you            to group meetings!**

**Figure 8.**  Conflict Log cover and directions. (Permission to photocopy is granted.)

# SESSION TWO

**Material Required for Session Two**

- name tags (same as last week)
- masking tape circles on the floor
- snacks (variety is good . . . remember, snacks + number of members)
- blank poster board to record group rules generated by members
- duplicated material (prepared prior to Session Two):
    poster with Clear Communication Model outlined (Figure 11)
    Situations for Clear Communication Practice (Figure 12)
    Conflict Resolution Strategy Wheel (Figure 13)
- metal brads or string for centers of Strategy Wheels
    Construct one Conflict Resolution Strategy Wheel per group member. Remember to encourage children
    to use their Wheels both at home and at meetings.
    1. Photocopy both pages (spinner wheel and options wheel) of Figure 13—make one set per
        child. (Colored paper is a fun choice.)
    2. Paste photocopies onto thin cardboard. (Old file folders make inexpensive sturdy Wheels.)
    3. Cut away excess so that only circles are left.
    4. On each spinner wheel, cut away window as indicated.
    5. Lay spinner wheel on top of options wheel and fasten together with metal brad or string.

**Session Time: 1 1/2 Hours**

**Goals for Session Two**

- to strengthen underlying structure and comforting group routine,
- to relate members' learning to their real-life experiences, and
- to teach and practice a model for clear communication.

# ACTIVITIES FOR SESSION TWO

**First 15 Minutes**

---
### Activity 2.1  DEVELOPING GROUP RULES
---

Have children sit in sub-team circles. Each team leader takes attendance and helps the team come up with a group rule. All teams bring rules to the facilitator and a poster is made with group rules. All members pledge to stick to the rules for the next 90 minutes. Figure 9 is an example of "Group Rules" that might be developed. These should be recorded on a poster board too and made visible during all sessions.

> **Group Rules:**
>
> 1. OK to share/pass
>
> 2. Show respect
>
> 3. Keep promises
>
> 4. Confidentiality

**Figure 9.** Group rules.

**Next 30 Minutes**

| **Activity 2.2  VALIDATING MEMBER EFFORTS** |
| --- |

Begin the session by praising members for keeping their commitments (coming back this week and recording conflicts in their logs).

| **Activity 2.3  PROBING CONFLICT LOG ENTRIES** |
| --- |

Lead the processing of recorded incidents in logs.  Some probes are shown in Figure 10.

> 1. Who was involved?
>
> 2. What was the issue?
>
> 3. What were the feelings?
>
> 4. What strategies were tried?
>
> 5. What worked?
>
> 6. What didn't work?

**Figure 10.** Probing questions.

---

### Activity 2.4  INTRODUCING THE CLEAR COMMUNICATION MODEL

---

Many strategies for resolving conflicts are available, and most of these strategies require communication skills. Clear communication is the key to much good problem solving. You, as facilitator, say, "Let's look at this model." (The model is shown in Figure 11.) This model should be made into a poster with wording large enough for all to read when displayed. Discuss the Clear Communication Model. Help the children understand each part and what it does. Give examples illustrating the times when using the model would be most effective.

I feel _____

when _____

I want _____

I'm willing to _____

_____

**Figure 11.** Clear Communication Model.

---

### Activity 2.5  PRACTICING CLEAR COMMUNICATION

---

Give a list of simulated opportunities about which to communicate. The list entitled "Situations for Clear Communication Practice" (Figure 12) represents situations in which communication may be the key to resolving conflict. Each member should have the chance to practice using the Clear Communication Model (Figure 11), inserting specifics pertinent to the situation.

**Next 30 Minutes**

---

### Activity 2.6  INTRODUCING THE CONFLICT RESOLUTION STRATEGY WHEEL

---

Introduce the "Conflict Resolution Strategy Wheel" (Figure 13). Discuss what it contains. The outside rim lists approaches (strategies) that may be used in a conflict. The window provides examples of verbal expression that might be useful when employing the corresponding strategy.

Members can brainstorm about different strategies with the conflict examples that they record in their Conflict Logs—real-life examples. Consulting the Strategy Wheel, they can examine the wording in the window to evaluate the possible effectiveness of the suggested verbal expression. As facilitator, offer information and clarification as the members discuss the Strategy Wheel. This is also an ideal time to discuss strategy selection (i.e., avoid, postpone, cooperate, etc.) for specific situations.

---

### Activity 2.7  SNACK TIME

---

Again, create a situation where number of crackers does not equal number of sub-team members. The team leaders of this session facilitate discussion on generating options for problem resolution.

**Last 15 Minutes**

---

### Activity 2.8  USING THE STRATEGY WHEEL WITH CONFLICT LOG ENTRIES

---

Use the Conflict Resolution Strategy Wheel to aid discussion of conflicts recorded in the Conflict Logs during last week. Look at who was involved. What was the conflict about? What were the differing perspectives? What feelings were evident? Did the people in conflict employ a strategy? If so, which one? Did it work? What would you have tried if you had been involved in the conflict? How would you have felt?

As a whole group, talk about what kinds of conflicts are hardest to deal with. How do we usually feel in conflict? Which strategy do we usually employ?

**Homework**

Have children record TV or "real" conflicts in their Conflict Logs this week.

**Possible Closing Ritual**

---

### Activity 2.9  SINGING TOGETHER

---

Sing "Let There Be Peace on Earth" or another closing ritual song.

# EVALUATION CONSIDERATIONS (WHAT TO LOOK FOR)

- Did all participants use their Conflict Logs as suggested?
- Are participants beginning to recognize the parts of a conflict?
- Is the number of strategies mentioned in discussion growing?
- Do you notice that child examples are becoming more personal? Be sure you are empathetic and provide privacy for individuals as appropriate (i.e., family violence witnessed by a child).
- How was snack time handled? Are group members showing creativity in resolving the "fun" problem of not enough to go around? If a child consistently chooses the same strategy each time, suggest an option.
- Are you making use of your sub-team leaders for taking attendance, leading snack discussion and distribution, and alerting you to possible teaching moments as conflicts naturally arise within teams?
- Are you watching siblings watching each other? Make sure you use specific praise and loud and clear so brother may have the opportunity to see sister in a new light or vice versa. For example, "Your clear communication statement of feelings and wants was *so* effective, George. I know your sister would *really* hear you if you tried that strategy at home!"
- And as always, how was the level of engagement? If a group member tends toward self-isolation, chat privately with his/her sub-team leader and encourage the drawing out of the isolated child with key roles in activities such as holding a poster, demonstrating the Conflict Resolution Strategy Wheel, or thinking of a new problem-solving strategy for snack time. However, the activities usually engage all so it is difficult to self-isolate.
- Are the sub-team leaders rotating? Make sure that each week there is a new leader in each sub-team. You can make this easy on yourself by having the leader from last week move a sticky star down to the next name on the attendance list for each sub-team. The names on the list can be written oldest to youngest, allowing the smaller child to experience the role-modeling of the older leaders before the younger child's week to lead comes up.

# SITUATIONS FOR CLEAR
# COMMUNICATION PRACTICE

- A "friend" is calling you names on the playground. What do you say?

- Your mom tells you to clean up your room five minutes before you have to leave for school. What do you say?

- Your sister/brother borrows your things without asking. What do you say?

- Your parent nags you about taking out the trash. What do you say?

- A kid on the playground hogs the tether ball and you want it. What do you say?

- You want to watch a certain TV program. No one else does. You have one TV in your home. What do you say?

- Your teacher is upset with you for not doing your homework. What do you say?

- You need to do homework at the baby-sitter's (day care). You never get around to it. What do you say?

- A kid at school takes your equipment when you are trying to play. What do you say?

- Your parent doesn't like that you talk back. What do you say?

**Figure 12.** Situations for clear communication practice.

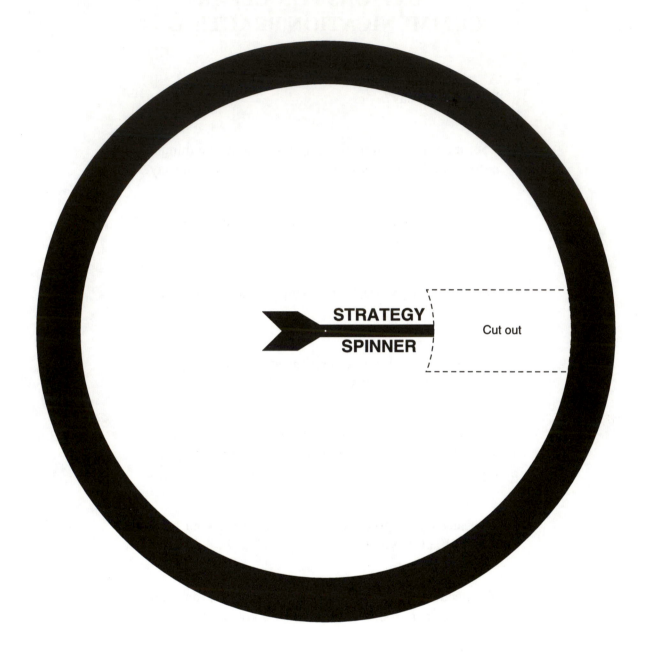

**Figure 13.** Conflict Resolution Strategy Wheel.

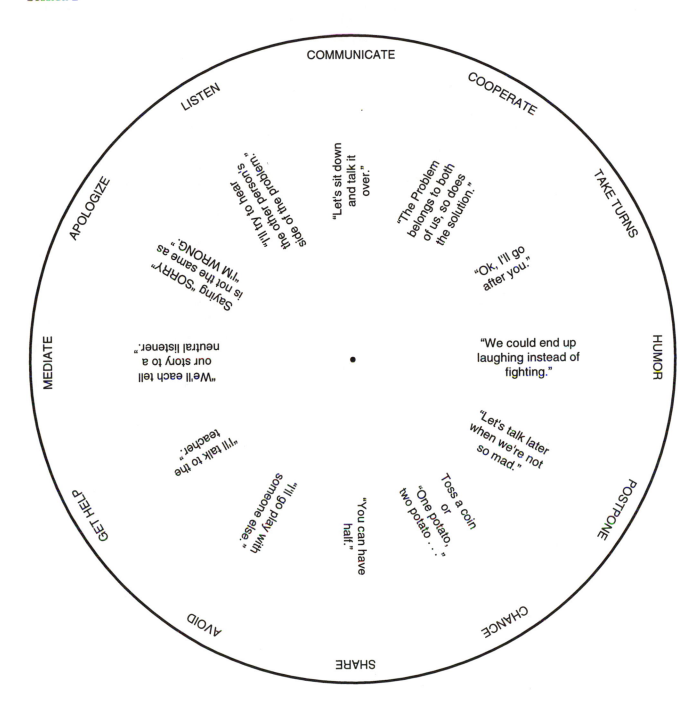

**Figure 13.** Continued.

# SESSION THREE

**Materials Required for Session Three**

- name tags
- masking tape circles on the floor
- chairs for role-play
- snacks
- poster about Ways to Listen (Figure 14)
- duplicated material (prepared prior to Session Three):
    - role-playing situations (Figures 15 and 16)
    - Mediator's Guide (Figure 17)
    - video (mediation or problem-solving)
    - mediator ID badges or banners (optional) (Figure 18)
- Strategy Wheels (Figure 13)

**Session Time: 1 1/2 Hours**

**Goals for Session Three**

- to introduce and practice mediation (a peer model used in schools—two peer mediators assisting two disputants in resolving their own problem),
- to bring learning about conflict close to the children's everyday experiences—especially school experiences, and
- to empower members in employing communication skills to assist disputing peers.


# ACTIVITIES FOR SESSION THREE

Have children sit in circles. Each sub-team leader takes attendance and renews commitments of the members to the group rules.


**First 30 Minutes**


| Activity 3.1  PROCESSING CONFLICT LOG ENTRIES |
|---|

Begin by having sub-team leaders process recorded conflict incidents from their Conflict Logs. The probing questions could be made available to the members to assist them in processing (Figure 10).


| Activity 3.2  DISCUSSING LISTENING SKILLS |
|---|

Begin by showing the listening skills poster (Figure 14) on ways we listen with our whole bodies, not just our ears. Have the whole group discuss what it feels like when you are not being listened to. How do we really know when someone is listening?

**Figure 14.** Ways to listen.


What part might listening skills play in conflict resolution?  If you can communicate clearly and listen effectively, do you think your chances of resolving conflicts successfully might increase?

---

### Activity 3.3  ROLE-PLAYING CONFLICTS

---

Have children draw role-play parts (Figure 15) and play out conflicts in teams, with other teams observing and leading the processing.  Remind children that they can use their Strategy Wheels during role-plays and at home between meetings.


**Second 30 Minutes**

---

### Activity 3.4  SHARING ABOUT TV CONFLICTS

---

Using the Conflict Resolution Strategy Wheel as a reference, invite sharing about the TV conflicts the members recorded in their Conflict Logs during the week.  The same format for analyzing the incidents as was used in Session Two (Figure 10) may be used here.  This sharing may be done in the whole group or in teams with the team leader modeling the facilitator's guidance.

---
**Activity 3.5  ENJOYING SNACK TIME**
---

By now, the children will look forward to the snack time and to the solving of a mini-conflict.  You will need to create the mini-conflict situation each time.

**Last 30 Minutes**

---
**Activity 3.6  VIEWING A PEER MEDIATION VIDEO**
---

There are many appropriate videos that are ideal for introducing the concept of mediation in which disputing children seek a neutral person who listens to each of their perspectives in turn and facilitates the process of their cooperative problem solving.  Many schools have their own training videos for Peer Mediation, which is a program modeled after the San Francisco's Community Board's original Conflict Manager model.  The community mediation service in any community will be pleased to have a group facilitator borrow their mediation training film as was done when this group was first initiated.  It was helpful for the group members to see "kids just like them" resolving playground disputes with the help of a peer.

Some suggestions of videos that are easily accessible are offered here:

Terros Peer Mediation Training Video
Terros, Inc., 711 E. Missouri
Phoenix, AZ  85014

Mediation in the Schools Video
N.A.M.E., 205 Hampshire House UMass
Amherst, MA  01003

Negotiating Skills for Kids, The Guidance Club Videos
Ready Reference Press, P.O. Box 5249
Santa Monica, CA  90409
San Francisco Community Board C.R. Resources for Schools & Youth

Peer Mediation Training Video, 149 Ninth Street
San Francisco, CA  94103

Conflict Resolution, Sunburst Publication Inc.
39 Washington Avenue, P. O. Box 40
Pleasantville, NY  10570-0040

After seeing and processing a peer mediation video, group members will be eager to practice mediation.  Role-plays are drawn (Figure 16), and some members volunteer to be mediators and some, disputants.  The "Mediator's Guide" (Figure 17) will be helpful for first-time mediators.  "Mediator ID Banners" or "Badges" (Figure 18) may add to the energy of the process if you choose to create and distribute either or both.  Again, remind children to use their Strategy Wheels during role-plays and during at-home, real-life conflict.

**Activity 3.7  TIME TO PROCESS**

Following the experience in the role-plays, you may wish to make a 'round-the-group check on feelings of mediators and disputants.  Questions like the following may assist this processing:

What did it feel like to help solve someone else's problem?

Were you able to guide those people in discovering their own solutions?

Did you experience any impatience when you could see a possible solution and the disputants could not?

As a disputant, what was your attitude toward the mediator?

Did the mediator reflect your feelings as well as the content of your responses?

If this had been a real mediation, do you think you would have felt that the problem had been resolved?

**Homework**

Instruct children for this week, to record in their Conflict Logs an instance when they use reflective listening skills.

**Possible Closing Ritual**

**Activity 3.8  SINGING A SONG TOGETHER**

Sing "Let There Be Peace on Earth" or another peaceful song.

## EVALUATION CONSIDERATIONS (WHAT TO LOOK FOR)

- Did the members learn the mediation format?  Were they able to keep their role-plays going with the help of the peer mediators' questions and reflections?
- Did as many children get the chance to take the role of mediator/disputant as possible?  If not, try to attend to this during the next session.
- Was a Conflict Resolution Strategy Wheel close by for easy reference as the role-plays evolved?
- Did you provide enough time to process role-plays?
- Some children will take great comfort in the more formal problem-solving model of peer mediation.  Many will wish to go home and mediate for Mom and Dad's fights.  Help members understand when their services as a mediator might be appropriate (playground, neighborhood peer dispute, etc.).
- The experience of role-playing a disputant is as valuable as being a mediator.
- The disputant's role develops perspective-taking, ability to identify emotions, and the capacity to empathize.  The mediator's role offers the child the opportunity to distance himself/herself from the conflict and, from that perspective, begin assisting disputants in generating possible options for dispute resolution.  The skill of reflecting feeling and content is obviously of value to all developing communicators.

# CONFLICT RESOLUTION
# ROLE-PLAYS

- Two friends are teasing you about your new haircut at recess. Recess is almost over. What do you say? What do you do?

- A bigger boy is pushing you and trying to fight with you on the way home from school. What do you say? What do you do?

- Your brother makes a new friend of the new boy on the block. You and your brother used to play together, and now he doesn't have time for you. He is busy running out the door to go to his new friend's house. What do you say? What do you do?

- Your mom has asked you nicely to clean up your room before she gets home from work. Now she is home and is getting really mad at you. What do you say? What do you do?

- Your dad and mom are divorced. Dad says he'll pick you up on the weekend and at the last minute calls to cancel. What do you say? What do you do?

- You come home from school to find your little sister in your private stuff drawer in your room. She has made a mess. What do you say? What do you do?

**Figure 15.** Sample role-plays for Activity 3.3.

# SIMULATIONS

- Your little brother is listening in on your phone conversations with your boyfriend/girlfriend. You catch him. What do you do? What do you say?

- Your stepdad wants you to help him in the yard this weekend, but your friend is having a sleep-over. You already have told your stepdad that you will help him. What do you say when your friend calls to ask if you are coming? What do you do?

- Your teacher has asked you to watch your behavior in music class. A kid in class always makes you laugh at the wrong time. You decide to talk to that kid. When do you do it? What do you say?

- Your teacher blames you for doing something you didn't do. You decide to talk to her. When do you do it? What do you say?

- Your sports coach says that you are not being a good sport because you got mad when you didn't get to play in the last game. You feel mad. You decide to talk to him. When do you do it? What do you say?

- You really hurt your dad's feelings by something you said. Do you avoid and hope he'll forget it? Or, do you decide to talk to him about it? If you talk, what to you say?

- Someone in your family has begun to drink too much. You are worried and scared. Do you hold in your feelings? Do you choose to talk about it? If you talk, to whom? And, when? What do you say?

- You have a conflict within yourself. You forgot to study for the test, and you can see the student's paper in front of you. What will you say to yourself? What will you do?

**Figure 16.** Sample role-plays for Activity 3.6.

## MEDIATOR'S GUIDE

1. Do you want to solve this problem?    Yes    No    (#1 disputant)

                                           Yes    No    (#2 disputant)

2. Do you agree to keep the group rules?    Yes    No    (#1)

                                           Yes    No    (#2)

3. (To #1)  Please tell your story.  You will not be interrupted.  (Reflect, Summarize)

4. (To #2)  Thank you for waiting patiently.  Please tell your story.  (Reflect, Summarize)

5. (To #1)  How did you feel?  (Reflect)

6. (To #2)  How did you feel?  (Reflect)

7. In what ways could this problem be solved?  (Reflect)

8. How many possible solutions can you come up with?  (Reflect)

9. (To #1)  What are you willing to do?  (Reflect)

10. (To #2)  What are you willing to do?  (Reflect)

11. Which of these options represents the best solution?

12. Which option do you feel would work the best?

13. It sounds like you have an agreement that could be worded like: _____.

14. Do you think this conflict is resolved?    Yes    No    (#1 disputant)

                                           Yes    No    (#2 disputant)

15.  Congratulations, you have resolved your problem.  Please tell your friends the dispute has been resolved.

**Figure 17.**  Mediator's guide used as a sequence check for beginning mediators.

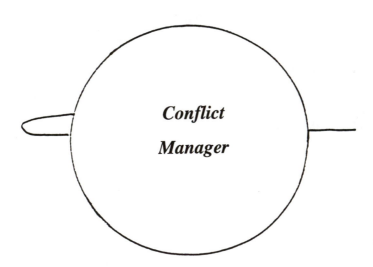

**Figure 18.** Mediator ID banner and badge ideas.

# SESSION FOUR

**Materials Required for Session Four**

- all materials/tools from pervious sessions available for group members to choose amongst when planning demonstrations
- snacks
- video (communication, problem solving)
- Conflict Logs
- clipboard for facilitator to record the sequence of group members' evolving demonstration plans for next session (demonstration for families)

**Session Time: 1 1/2 Hours**

**Goals for Session Four**

- to summarize knowledge about conflict and strategies learned,
- to review all concepts learned and activities experienced,
- to plan a demonstration for parents in which each child will have several integral parts or roles, and
- to "physicalize" the increasing ownership of the group by the members.


# ACTIVITIES FOR SESSION FOUR


Have children sit in team circles. Each team leader takes attendance and renews commitments of members to the group rules.


**First 45 Minutes**


| Activity 4.1  SUMMARIZING USE OF "TOOLS" OF CONFLICT RESOLUTION |
|---|

Begin the session by having the children summarize all the ways of resolving conflict that the group has learned and practiced over the last three sessions.


| Activity 4.2  VIEWING A PROBLEM-SOLVING VIDEO |
|---|

Your selection and presentation of a video in which the group members can identify the various problem-solving strategies they have been talking about in the sessions could be appropriate at this time. Again, videos are available for Problem Solving, Getting Along, and Negotiating topics. A classic children's film in which conflict plays a leading role also can serve as a way for group members to see others using (or not using) the very strategies they have learned and practiced over the last three sessions. After watching the video, lead a discussion on the video content, emphasizing the children's accumulated knowledge and growing "expert status."

---
### Activity 4.3  DISCUSSING THE HOMEWORK
---

You may choose to have team leaders guide the discussion of Conflict Log homework from last week.  You may want to emphasize that the skills and the group procedure now belong more to the members than to yourself (the facilitator).

**Last 45 Minutes**

---
### Activity 4.4  SELECTING "SCENES" FOR DEMONSTRATION
---

Have group members select which skills or activities they would like to demonstrate for their families at the end of the last session.  Team leaders can get individual commitments, and time can be given for the children to "organize" the sequence and content of their demonstration.  This is an opportunity for you as facilitator to step back as children personalize their conflict resolution skills and reinforce ownership of not only the demonstration, but of the group experience as well.

As group members plan their demonstration, you may act as roving consultant and make sure all the materials (ropes, Strategy Wheels, Mediator Banners, posters, clipboards, snacks, etc.) are available for the children as reminders of moments significant to them.

You, as facilitator, should not be surprised if the children plan to run their parents through the activities and even ask their families to divide an inadequate number of cookies amongst themselves in a way that promotes communication and reduces conflict.  You might count on a tug-of-war, a narrator, and several role-plays using clear communication and reflective listening.  It almost can be assumed that the children will choose to end their demonstration by singing "Let There Be Peace on Earth" (or other song) for their guests.

## EVALUATION CONSIDERATIONS (WHAT TO LOOK FOR)

- Did each child come up with something she/he wished to share with parents?

     Some ideas:

> A child holds a poster illustrating listening and shows parents how to listen with whole self.
>
> A child gives snacks to parents and asks them to cooperatively solve the problem of not enough to go around.
>
> Children do tug-of-war and speaker (narrator) identifies this as a competitive strategy and asks the losers how they might feel if they had to solve all problems competitively.
>
> A child demonstrates the Conflict Resolution Strategy Wheel and explains each strategy.
>
> Four children role-play a mediation (2 disputants, 2 mediators).
>
> Two children Tied-Up-in-Knots tell about the importance of communication when "bound" by a common or shared problem.

- What is the engagement level of the members?  My experience has been that all are very busy planning and practicing, and require only momentary consults with me as I circulate around the room.
- Don't forget snack time.  If you do, they'll remind you, but ritual and routine offer security as they become more and

more independent owners of their new conflict resolution skills.

- Keep a good record of the sequence of their demonstration so that at the last session all can go smoothly as you cue each subsequent demonstration.

- Observe! This is the first time that the members are working with any member from any sub-team. They are choosing to work together on the basis of common interest and expertise. "Oh, I'm a good mediator and so are you, Sue. Let's do a role-play for our demonstration." This is wonderful as they are showing you what concepts "stuck" with them or what social skills have been enhanced by the task approach.

- There are enough concepts and demonstration ideas to go around for everybody. A natural conflict resolution opportunity may arise when two members pick the same idea. Use this. Find a volunteer mediator; generate options. Praise them for using what they have learned to solve real-life conflicts.

# SESSION FIVE

**Materials Required for Session Five**

- all posters and tools from previous sessions
- refreshments for parents and children (optional)
- facilitator's clipboard record of planned demonstration sequence
- duplicated material (prepared prior to Session Five):
  - post-group survey for younger children (Figure 4)
  - post-group survey for older children (Figure 5)
  - Conflict Manager Diplomas (Figure 19)
  - group evaluation forms for parents/guardians (Figure 20)

**Session Time:  1 1/2 Hours**

**Goals for Session Five**

- to review and present a summary of learned concepts and skills;
- to demonstrate for parents/guardians/families—encouraging the generalization of skills to the home setting; and
- to help parents/guardians recognize the empowerment of group members—celebrating their accomplishment to facilitate group closure.

# ACTIVITIES FOR SESSION FIVE

**First 30 Minutes**

---

### Activity 5.1  REHEARSING DEMONSTRATIONS

---

Group members repeat their opening ritual in their circles and then go about rehearsing their "demonstration of skills."

Keep parents busy by offering refreshments, as this session can be a social celebration for the children and their families.

**Last 60 Minutes**

---

### Activity 5.2  DEMONSTRATING SKILLS LEARNED FOR FAMILIES

---

When group members are ready, the demonstration ensues.  You may wish to sit back and enjoy the children's teaching of what they have learned—their sharing of what they have experienced.  Your attention may be on the physical space and prop requirements and comfort of the observers.

---

### Activity 5.3  DISTRIBUTING DIPLOMAS (Figure 19)

---

The children appreciate individual attention to their graduation as conflict managers.  This is your opportunity to say something special about the growth of each individual member as you hand out diplomas.  The diploma ceremony is very important and one that parents/guardians appreciate.

---

### Activity 5.4  ADMINISTERING EVALUATION FORMS

---

After the children have finished their demonstrations, use the form provided (Figure 20) and ask parents/guardians to give you feedback.  This feedback is necessary in that it helps facilitation improve each time and helps ensure that needs of members are addressed specifically.

---

### Activity 5.5  ADMINISTERING POST-GROUP SURVEYS

---

After the children have finished their demonstrations, administer the post-group surveys (Figures 4 and 5).  The parents/guardians can complete their group evaluations (Figure 20) at the same time, or socializing and refreshments can occupy adults while children respond to the conflict attitude survey to assess attitudinal shifts that may have taken place as a result of the group experience.

You may wish to enlist a helper to assist children in focusing on their post-group surveys when the climate is one of celebration.

Once you have the pre- and post-group responses, comparisons of attitudes toward conflict and self-perception of ability to deal with conflict can be made.

## EVALUATION CONSIDERATIONS (WHAT TO LOOK FOR)

- Did each child appear satisfied with his/her contribution to the demonstration?
- Was there a festive air?
- Did parents/guardians respond positively to the demonstration and to their child's part in it?
- Did parents/guardians ask good questions?
- Did you praise parents/guardians for making their child's growth possible (the transportation commitment)?
- Did members ask to keep some physical memorabilia from the group experience?  For example, a child who was desperately attached to the Clear Communication Model poster (I feel _____ when _____.  I want _____.  I'm willing to _____.) may want to take it home so "everybody will really listen" to one another at home.
- Did you have members complete the post-group survey following the demonstration?
- Comparing the pre- and post-group measures will give you a sense of confidence as you discover that those who once thought that conflict was bad, now see it as a natural part of life and something to manage rather that something to erase.

- When the members were completing their post-group surveys, were the parents/guardians completing the Group Evaluation for Parents?  This produces interesting results.  Your members have already brought their learning home, and the parent evaluation will make this clear.
- If this has been an effective group, you probably found yourself less necessary to the process as the weeks progressed.  This is a good sign that your early attention to structure, ritual, and materials has produced the "ownership" and member-empowerment desirable in most group development.
- If, when you are walking out of the building, you hear a parent ask a small group member, "Well, what did you learn?" and the child replies, "I learned how to play tug-of-war!", don't despair.  His/hers was a holistic experience that developed on many levels over five weeks.  His/her conflict resolution skills will be tested on the playground and at home, and part of the *Conflict Resolution for Kids* group experience will be there too, helping him/her transform obstacles into opportunities.

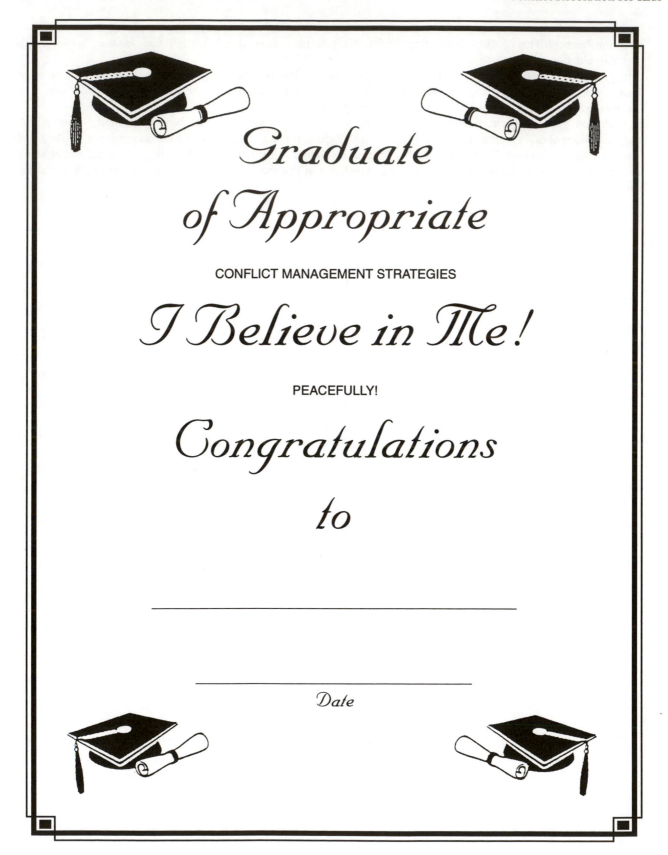

**Figure 19.** Sample of a Conflict Manager Diploma.  (Permission is given to photocopy.)

## GROUP EVALUATION FOR PARENTS/GUARDIANS

1. How do you feel generally about the group, CONFLICT RESOLUTION FOR KIDS?

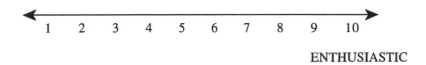

ENTHUSIASTIC

2. How does (do) your child (children) feel about the group?

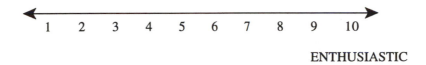

ENTHUSIASTIC

3. Would you like to see more children's groups offered?    YES    NO

4. Was the time convenient for you?    YES    NO

5. Was the location convenient for you?    YES    NO

6. What was the most important thing your child learned from his/her experience in this group?

_____

7. Do you have any comments for this facilitator?

_____

_____

8. Would you involve your child in other social skills groups in the future?    YES    NO

9. What topics for future groups would benefit your child (children)?

_____

**Thank you for your time and participation!**

**Figure 20.** Group evaluation form for parents/guardians.  (Permission is given to photocopy.)

# CONCLUSION

Having endeavored to offer a suggested format for developing and implementing a conflict resolution training group for children, the author hopes that facilitators in various settings may personalize the format and content and by so doing, end up with an experience that works in their specific settings. The following information will touch on the attitude survey responses that resulted from one personal experience as facilitator of such a group. Responses to the Schmidt and Friedman (1985) survey (Figure 5), which was completed by four older children in a group of nine, are summarized in Figure 21.

Comparing the pre- and post-group surveys, it may be that these older children (11 to 13 years of age) had a broader view of conflict as a natural and unavoidable part of life. From their answers on items 4 and 20, after the group experience they seem to view conflict as something to manage rather than eliminate. This apparent shift in attitude may be due in part to having gathered more information about conflict resolution strategies and having had the opportunity to process feelings about conflict in a safe, nurturing environment. Further research could explore a possible cause-effect relationship.

Five younger children (6 to 10 years of age) were part of the study group. Their pre- and post-group survey results can be summarized as follows: In the younger children, too, an apparent shift away from the bad/good aspects of conflict can be noted. A possible improvement in personal confidence in ability to manage conflict is reflected in all but one of these five youngsters (see Figure 22).

In evaluating the success of the group, it is important to elicit comments from the parents/guardians as well. Though they do not participate in each activity, they hear the comments on the way home in the car, and they feel the spirit of the group room. A sample parent evaluation is included in this guidebook illustrating possible questions to ask parents/guardians (Figure 20). I hope that you choose to employ this tool each time a final group meeting is held. Also included are ideas for visual aids that hopefully you chose to have on display at every group meeting (Figure 3). These items add to the atmosphere and focus of the group room and also become tools for demonstration. Parents/guardians will notice and appreciate these.

The author hopes that a group facilitator was able to pick up this guide and discover some basic information about conflict resolution for kids, some simple tools, and a useful outline for session activities. Such basics are easily personalized, and readers of this guide are encouraged to add and subtract, embellish and simplify, as their personal and professional experience suggests.

### GROUP CONFLICT SURVEY RESULTS

| Pre-group | | Post-group |
|---|---|---|
| 2T  2F | 1.  Conflict is a natural part of life. | 4T  0F |
| 1T  3F | 2.  All conflicts end in violence. | 0T  4F |
| 2T  2F | 3.  There are at least two sides in every conflict. | 4T  0F |
| 4T  0F | 4.  It is possible to eliminate conflict. | 0T  4F |
| 4T  0F | 5.  Behavior can be either appropriate or inappropriate depending on where it happens. | 4T  0F |
| 4T  0F | 6.  Inappropriate behavior can cause conflict. | 4T  0F |
| 1T  3F | 7.  Behavior cannot be changed. | 0T  4F |
| 2T  2F | 8.  People all over the world have the same basic needs. | 4T  0F |
| 3T  1F | 9.  Unmet needs can cause conflict. | 4T  0F |
| 3T  1F | 10.  There are many nonviolent alternatives available to solve a conflict. | 4T  0F |
| 4T  0F | 11.  It is not possible for everyone to win a conflict. | 0T  4F |
| 2T  2F | 12.  Calling someone a name is a form of violence. | 4T  0F |
| 2T  2F | 13.  Frustration always leads to violence. | 0T  4F |
| 3T  1F | 14.  It is important to learn not to get angry. | 0T  4F |
| 0T  4F | 15.  Adults never have conflicts. | 0T  4F |
| 1T  3F | 16.  Conflict can be constructive as well as destructive. | 4T  0F |
| 3T  1F | 17.  Conflicts can escalate or de-escalate, depending on what is said or done. | 4T  0F |
| 2T  2F | 18.  Fighting fair means respect for others and for ourselves. | 4T  0F |
| 2T  2F | 19.  In resolving a conflict it is important not to embarrass or humiliate the other person. | 4T  0F |
| 2T  2F | 20.  Learning to handle conflict constructively takes a lot of practice and skill. | 4T  0F |

**Figure 21.**  Comparison of pre- and post-group survey responses (older children).

**GROUP CONFLICT SURVEY RESULTS**

Pre-group        Directions: Color 🙂 if you think it is true.        Post-group

| Pre-group | | | Post-group |
|---|---|---|---|
| 2T 3F | 🙂 | 1. Conflict is part of life. | 5T 0F |
| 5T 0F | 🙂 | 2. All conflict is bad. | 1T 4F |
| 3F 2T | 🙂 | 3. Ways to solve conflicts can be learned. | 5T 0F |
| 5F 0T | 🙂 | 4. Talking and listening are ways to solve problems. | 5T 0F |
| 3F 2T | 🙂 | 5. I can learn to manage conflict. | 4T 1F |

**Figure 22.** Comparison of pre- and post-group survey responses (younger children).

# BIBLIOGRAPHY

Duncan, J.A., & Gumaer, J. (1980). *Development groups for children.* Springfield, IL: Charles C. Thomas.

Gazda, G., Asbury, F., Childers, W., & Walters, R. (1977). *Human relations development: A manual for educators.* Boston: Allyn & Bacon.

Koch, M. (1988). Resolving disputes: Students can do it better. *NASSP Bulletin, 72*(504), 16-18.

Maxwell, J. (1989). Mediation in the schools. *Mediation Quarterly, 7,* 149-154.

Morganett, R. (1990). *Skills for living: Group counseling activities.* Indianapolis, IN: Research Press.

*Negotiating skills for kids video.* (1990). Santa Monica, CA: Guidance Club Publications.

*Peer mediation training video.* (1990). Phoenix, AZ: State Department of Education.

Schmidt, F., & Friedman, A. (1985). *Peace education for children.* Miami Beach, FL: Peace Education Foundation.

Seligman, M. (1982). *Group psychotherapy and counseling with special populations.* Baltimore, MD: University Park Press.

Terros, Inc. (1988). *School mediation project training manual.* Phoenix, AZ: Community Mediation Publications.

Yalom, I.D. (1985). *The theory and practice of group psychotherapy* (3rd ed.). New York: Basic Books.

# ABOUT THE AUTHOR

Pam Lane has taught elementary school students—with and without special needs—for 15 years. She received her bachelor's degree in English literature and theatre arts in 1975 from College of Notre Dame in the San Francisco Bay area. After completing California's Teacher Education program, she began teaching third grade and later, Kindergarten. It was while teaching Kindergarten in a migrant community in Southern California that Pam developed an interest in children with special needs. She received her master's degree in special education from Arizona State University in 1982.

Pam moved back to Arizona and spent 10 years in the Paradise Valley School District teaching special education students and first graders. During this period, she became interested in the power of peers to positively influence each other. Pam developed classroom programs to engender prosocial skill development: "Can Do Kids" and "Helping Hands" were among her creative projects emphasizing cooperative learning.

Over her seven years with first graders, Pam began to notice changes in six-year-olds. Her observations led her to believe that due to changes in the structure of the family, children were not receiving the required emotional support that would allow them to adapt to change effectively. School counseling often was reserved for middle school and older students. Prevention and intervention at an earlier age made sense to Pam. In 1992 she graduated from Arizona State's master's in counseling program. It was at this time that Pam left the public school system to address the emotional and behavioral development of children in social service, hospital, and community health settings.

In each of these settings, *Conflict Resolution for Kids* was developed and field-tested. Pam's training as a Family Mediator and community service work with the Arizona Attorney General's office of Court Mediation influenced her work with children, emphasizing cooperative rather than competitive ways of resolving conflict. Her experience in education, counseling, and conflict resolution provided the motivation for developing a group experience for children offering social skills training in communication and dispute resolution.

Pam, obviously a believer in life-span development, currently is pursuing a Ph.D. in educational psychology with a developmental emphasis. Pam sums up her philosophy of conflict like this: Children learn from models. If their models only have one tool for conflict resolution—a hammer—then the violent and litigious nature of our society will continue to predominate. However, with a bigger tool chest, packed with a variety of strategic tools for addressing interpersonal disputes, our children will become more confident, effective problem-solvers who know how to attack the problem without attacking the person in the process. Pam's *Conflict Resolution for Kids: A Facilitator's Guide* is offered in the spirit of optimism about our children's potential to positively affect future society.

# GROUP FACILITATOR'S EXPERIENCE USING THIS GUIDE

## *Conflict Resolution for Kids*

1. The materials provided were useful.


1----------2----------3----------4----------5--------6---------7-------8-------9-------10


2. I incorporated the following types of materials easily into the existing group format: _____

_____


1----------2----------3----------4----------5--------6---------7-------8-------9-------10


3. The group structure assisted concept and activity development.


1----------2----------3----------4----------5--------6---------7-------8-------9-------10


4. The setting in which I used the book was:

_____

5. The population with which I worked (my group members) can be described as:

_____

6. The age range in my group was:

_____

7. The most helpful part of *Conflict Resolution for Kids: A Facilitator's Guide* was:

_____

8. I will/will not plan to facilitate this group again.  If not, my reasons being are:

_____


Please send to:  Pamela Lane, Arizona State University, Division of Psychology in Education, Tempe, AZ  85287-0611

## DATE DUE

| | | | |
|---|---|---|---|
| APR 2 7 1997 | | | |
| APR 2 6 1999 | | | |
| NOV 2 7 2000 | | | |
| | | | |
| | | | |
| | | | |
| | | | |
| | | | |
| | | | |
| | | | |
| | | | |
| | | | |
| | | | |
| | | | |
| | | | |
| | | | |
| | | | |
| | | | |
| GAYLORD | | | PRINTED IN U.S.A. |